BASEBALL

Andrew **S**antella

RIGBY
INTERACTIVE
LIBRARY

This edition © 1997 Rigby Education
Published by Rigby Interactive Library,
an imprint of Rigby Education,
division of Reed Elsevier, Inc.
500 Coventry Lane
Crystal Lake, IL 60014

Printed in the United States of America

00 99 98 97 96
10 9 8 7 6 5 4 3 2 1

Library of Congress Cataloging-in-Publication Data
Santella, Andrew.
    Baseball / Andrew Santella.
        p.   cm. — (Successful Sports)
    Includes index.
    Summary: Surveys the attitudes, skills, equipment, and tactics
involved in playing baseball well.
    ISBN 1-57572-068-X
    1. Baseball—Juvenile literature.   [1. Baseball.]   I. Title.   II. Series.
GV867.5.S27 1996
796.357—dc20
                                                                    96-7513
                                                                    CIP
                                                                    AC

Acknowledgments
The publishers would like to thank the following for permission to
reproduce photographs:
Allsport USA/Doug Pensinger: p. 29; Allsport USA/Jonathan Daniel: p. 10;
Allsport USA/Otto Greule: p. 5; AP/Wide World Photos: p. 18; Culver
Pictures, Inc.: pp. 23, 24, 25, 27; David Madison: pp. 6, 11, 15; John
Morrison: p. 19; Duomo/©Al Tielemans: p. 16; Duomo/©Bryan Yablonsky:
Front Cover; PhotoEdit/©David Young-Wolff: pp. 6, 12, 20; PhotoEdit/
©Tony Freeman: p. 16; Sports Photo Masters/Chuck Rydlewski: p. 14; Sports
Photo Masters/©Craig Melvin: copyright page; Sports Photo Masters/©Don
Smith: p. 17; Sports Photo Masters/©Jonathan Kirn: p. 21; Sports Photo
Masters/©Mitchell B. Reibel: pp. 2, 4, 8, 13, 28; UPI/Bettmann: p. 22, 26;

Illustrator: Stephen Brayfield: p. 9.

Visit Rigby's
Education Station®
on the
World Wide Web at
http://www.rigby.com

Contents

The National Pastime

BASEBALL FACTS

The first girl to appear in a Little League World Series played for Belgium in 1984. The first American girl played in 1989.

In 1846, the New York Nine beat the New York Knickerbockers 23 to 1 in the first ever official game of baseball. That game didn't decide any championships. Judging by the score, it probably wasn't even exciting to watch. But from that first game, baseball developed into America's **national pastime.** For 150 years, Americans have been playing, watching, and talking about baseball. That's a record no other sport can claim.

The Chicago White Sox' Frank Thomas is called the "Big Hurt" because his powerful swing can do great damage to the opposing team.

Today, it's not just Americans who love the game. More and more, people around the world have come to enjoy baseball. In fact, some of the best major-league players come from Latin American countries, such as Mexico and the Dominican Republic. Baseball is also popular in Japan and other Asian nations. In 1995, Japanese pitching star Hideo Nomo joined the Los Angeles Dodgers. His performance here wowed U.S. crowds.

More than 2 million young people in 23 countries compete in **Little League** baseball. Teams from Taiwan and other faraway nations are among the most competitive in the annual Little League World Series.

Why is America—and the rest of the world—so crazy about baseball? It's partly because baseball is a game of skill, and it's challenging. But it's also easy to learn, so just about anybody can play it. By comparison, watch a professional football or basketball game. Most of the players are enormous. Baseball rewards skill, not size. The biggest players may be **power hitters**, but the small players often are just as valuable for their speed or agility.

Baseball also has the perfect combination of offense and defense. For example, the bases are 90 feet apart in the **major leagues** (60 feet in Little League). If they were closer together, it would be too easy to reach base and too difficult to get batters **out**. The games would go on and on, and the scores would be high. But the rules of the game have made a perfect balance between offense and defense that keeps the game exciting.

Whatever the reasons for baseball's popularity, it's sure to be around for a long time to come. The sport may change over time, but at its heart baseball is still the game that was played back in 1846.

Greg Maddux of the Atlanta Braves may be the greatest pitcher in the game today.

BASEBALL FACTS

Baseball is one of the few sports played without a clock. That means the pace can seem to be slow. But that's part of baseball's appeal. Players, managers, and even fans can consider strategies between each pitch. This mental aspect of the game keeps baseball interesting, even when nothing appears to be happening.

Play Ball!

Before a game begins, the team's manager makes a **lineup.** The lineup tells who will play what position. It also tells the team's batting order.

Who's On First?

Every player on a team has a role to play to help the team. Managers make lineups with this in mind. Fast players who get on base a lot tend to bat first. Power hitters usually hit third or fourth. The idea is for the first batters to get on base and for the power hitters to drive them home.

STRIKE ZONE

Likewise, on defense, players are positioned according to skill. Every team sends onto the field a pitcher, a catcher, four infielders, and three outfielders. Because catching is physically demanding, a strong, sturdy player usually plays this position. Quick players, on the other hand, do well in the outfield. Also, left-handed players usually only play the outfield or first base, or they pitch. Of course there are exceptions to these rules. If a player is talented enough, he or she may play well at any position.

The strike zone extends from the armpits to the top of the knees of the batter and across home plate.

Sliding is one baseball skill that looks natural. But it, too, takes some practice.

Pitcher vs. Batter

The most important part of a baseball game is the battle between the pitcher and the batter. Even though baseball is a team game, all the action begins with this face-off. The goal of the batter is usually to reach base in whatever way possible. That can mean getting a **base hit** or drawing a **base on balls** (walking), or even being hit by a pitched ball. But sometimes, the batter has a special goal. For example, if there is a runner on third base, he or she may want to hit the ball on the fly to the outfield. This gives the base runner the chance to score by **tagging up** from third base.

For the pitcher, the goal is to get the batter out. Some pitchers may think this means throwing the ball as hard as possible. The problem is, if a pitcher thinks only about throwing hard, he or she may walk batters. Walks are as bad as hits. Often the best way to get batters out is to throw strikes. Even if the batter does hit the ball, the defensive players at least have a chance to make a play.

BASEBALL FACTS

It's always been "one, two, three strikes you're out," right? Sure, but some rules of baseball have changed over the years. In the 1800s, pitchers threw underhand, batters could request high or low pitches, and batters could walk on nine balls. By 1900, the rules were the same as today: four balls for a walk and three strikes you're out.

Getting into Gear

Baseball players need only a few pieces of equipment. But the right equipment allows a player to perform better, enjoy the game more, and avoid injuries.

On defense, there's the **fielder's glove.** Outfielders usually use larger gloves than infielders do. But no matter what the player's position, the glove has to fit. A glove that's too big can be difficult to control.

First basemen sometimes use gloves that are longer and shaped like a scoop. These gloves make it easier to catch low throws that skip along the ground. The catcher's glove is the biggest and most heavily padded glove. It also may be the hardest to get used to wearing and using. But practice helps catchers become comfortable with their gloves. Most youth teams supply players with a catcher's mitt. But players should have their own fielder's gloves.

Most teams also provide bats. Choosing the right bat is important. Many young players want to use the largest bat they can find. They believe that heavier bats will make the ball travel farther. But actually, it's more important to create speed with your swing. That's easiest to do with a bat that is light enough to swing without a lot of extra effort.

Always wear a helmet when batting and running the bases.

Players should always wear a helmet while batting and running the bases. The helmet should fit snugly, so it doesn't fly off. It also should have earflaps to protect the sides of the head and face. Wearing a helmet is the best protection for a player in the batter's box. It's not unusual for young players to be afraid of being hit by a pitch. A helmet can make players feel safer and more confident.

Catchers need the most equipment of any player, beginning with a face mask and helmet. The catcher's mask should include a throat guard. A chest protector and shin guards for the legs are also important. To be of any help, all this equipment needs to fit properly. Pads should fit snugly so that they offer protection but they shouldn't get in the way of playing.

And finally, there's the baseball: five ounces of yarn wound around a cork center, covered by horsehide and red stitches. No one can play ball without it.

Pointers

Injuries are no fun. Enjoy the game more by playing safely. Wear the right equipment and make sure it fits.

Field of Play

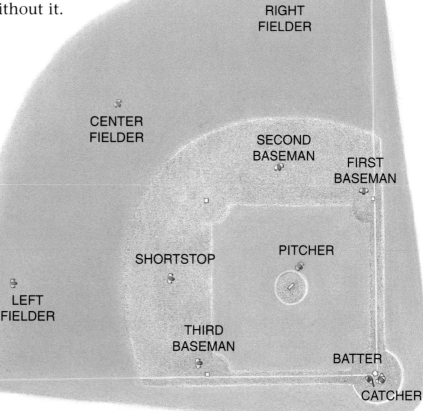

The field of play. In the major leagues, bases are 90 feet apart. They're 60 feet apart in Little League. The pitcher's mound is a little more than 60 feet from home plate in the big leagues. It's just 46 feet away in Little League.

RIGHT FIELDER

CENTER FIELDER

SECOND BASEMAN

FIRST BASEMAN

SHORTSTOP

PITCHER

LEFT FIELDER

THIRD BASEMAN

BATTER

CATCHER

Batter Up!

Some say that hitting a baseball is the most difficult task in all sports. Players with .300 **batting averages** are considered excellent hitters. Consider, however, that hitting .300 means that you only get 3 hits in 10 at-bats. So even the best hitters fail 7 times out of 10.

There are many grips, stances, and approaches to the ball that a batter can take. Sometimes it's hard to know which is best. Probably the most important thing for hitters is comfort. If a stance feels awkward, it probably won't lead to success.

Getting Ready

Most players grip the bat so that the tips of their fingers meet the palms of their hands. The bat should rest in the fingers, not the palms. The right and left hands should be touching each other, with no space between them.

Sluggers such as Juan Gonzalez make hitting look easy, but it is really one of the most challenging tasks in baseball.

Pointers

Bunting is one of the most overlooked skills in baseball. Even some major leaguers don't do it very well. But it's easy to learn and it's an effective way of getting on base or advancing your teammates from one base to another.

Watch the professionals and you'll see a wide variety of batting stances. Major-league players use a stance that is comfortable and that has worked over time. If you're just beginning to play, start with a basic stance. Place your back foot parallel to the back line of the **batter's box.** Place your front foot slightly ahead of your shoulder. Bend your knees slightly and distribute your weight equally on each foot. Hold your bat just above and behind your back shoulder.

It's important to use the proper stance when bunting.

Taking a Swing

When the pitcher begins to wind up, shift your weight to your back foot. When the ball is thrown, take a six-inch stride forward with your front foot. Make sure you do not move your hands and the bat forward when you stride.

If the pitch looks like one you can hit, begin your swing by pulling your hands forward toward the plate. Shift your weight to your front foot and push from your back foot. Rotate your hips as you move your hands, so that your hands and body move together. Keep your eye on the ball and try not to jerk your head as you swing. Follow through after you have made contact with the ball, and be ready to run.

Selecting good pitches is key to hitting. That means knowing the **strike zone.** The strike zone extends the width of home plate and from the batter's armpits to the top of the knees. By swinging at pitches only in the strike zone, you will improve your chances of hitting the ball.

Running the Bases

Being a good base runner has more to do with smart play than with speed. The best **base** runners plan ahead. That is, they know how many outs there are, what the score is, and who is playing in the field. Then, when the ball is hit, the runner knows exactly what to do.

Pointers

Good baserunning depends on alertness. Always know how many outs there are and keep one eye on your base coach. If you know how many outs there are, you can figure out ahead of time whether you should run or stay put when a fly ball is hit.

Make sure you touch each base as you round the bases.

Getting a Base Hit

When you hit a ground ball to the infield, take a direct route to first base and run through the base. As long as you don't turn toward second base, you can overrun first base. If you hit a ball into the outfield, swerve out into foul territory a bit as you approach first. This will help you turn the corner at first base. When you hit the ball into the outfield, turn the corner at first base and be prepared to run for second in case the outfielder drops or juggles the ball. Likewise, when running from first to third, run in a slight arc, so that you'll be able to turn the corner at full speed.

Moving Ahead

What you do on the **base paths** depends on the number of outs. With two outs, runners should always run as soon as the ball is hit. With fewer than two outs, it's more complicated. On fly balls, you should in most cases run about halfway to the next base, until you can see whether or not the outfielder will make the catch. If the catch is made, you'll have time to get back to your base. If the ball is dropped, you'll be able to advance.

If you're on third with one out, and the batter hits a fly ball, you may want to tag up. You must wait until the ball is caught before you can tag the base you're on and advance to the next base. Tagging up takes precise timing. If you leave too soon, you may be called out. If you leave too late, the outfielder may throw you out.

In a close play at any base, you should slide. Sliding allows you to get to the base quickly without overrunning it. You can slide on either side, but always slide early. You should hit the ground about five feet ahead of the base. If you wait too long before starting your slide, you may get injured.

Kenny Lofton's speed and baserunning has made him a valuable offensive player.

Pitching

The pitcher may be the most important player on the baseball field. He or she starts the action by delivering the ball to home plate. Some pitchers have been able to beat hitters by simply throwing the ball so hard that hitters can't hit it. Other pitchers win with the ability to pitch the ball exactly where they want it to go. A pitcher with both outstanding control and an excellent **fastball** is very hard to hit against.

Because the pitcher is involved in every play of the game and because pitching is so physically demanding, pitchers must prepare for their job. Before each game, stretching is important, as is warming up the arm. If a pitcher tries to throw as hard as possible without warming up first, he or she is certain to become injured.

Big Randy Johnson throws one of the hardest fastballs in the major leagues.

Throwing hard is not the only way to succeed as a pitcher. Controlling the location of your pitches is also important.

As in hitting, there are many ideas about how pitchers should grip the ball, wind up, and throw. A good, all-purpose grip has two-fingers positioned slightly apart across the seams of the ball. Begin your **windup** by stepping back with your glove-side foot. With your pitching hand holding the ball in your glove, bring your hands up over your head. Then place the foot on your pitching arm side in front of the **pitcher's rubber,** so you can use the rubber to push off.

With your hands still above your head, turn your body so you face third base if you are right-handed, first base if you are left-handed. Then raise the knee of your glove-side up toward your waist. Now bring your hands down, separating them as they reach your raised knee. Your pitching-arm hand should come up behind your hip. Then step toward the plate, pushing off from the rubber. Bring your pitching arm forward in an arc and release the ball from about eye-level. After releasing the ball, follow through with your pitching arm and square your body off to home plate. This will put you in position to field the ball if it is hit back to you.

BASEBALL FACTS

A curveball starts out heading at the batter, but then curves over the plate. A change-up looks like a fastball, but fools the batter, because it travels more slowly. A sinker drops just before it gets to home plate. A knuckleball, which is thrown with the fingertips, can fool even the catcher and pitcher.

Playing the Infield

Infielders have to be on their toes—or at least on the balls of their feet—at all times. A sharply hit ball can get to an infielder very quickly, so he or she has to be prepared. When you play the infield, stand with your weight slightly forward and on the balls of your feet. Keep your glove open and your knees bent.

Whether you play first base, second base, third base, or shortstop, stay alert and aware of the game situation. Before each pitch, you should know the number of outs and the position of the base runners. Then, when the ball is hit to you, you will already have planned what your play is.

If a ground ball is hit directly at you, charge it. Sitting back and waiting for it to come to you only gives the ball more opportunities to take funny hops. Or you may wait so long that the base runner will beat your throw.

Pointers

Managers and coaches teach infielders to keep their bodies in front of balls hit at them. In this way they are not reaching off to the side. Of course, that means some ground balls will bounce up and hit the infielder. Getting over the fear of being hit by a ground ball is not easy, but it's essential to becoming a good fielder.

To field a ground ball, bend your knees and keep your glove low.

The most common error young
players make is letting the ball get
underneath their gloves. Keep your glove
low to the ground and bend your knees to pick up
the ball. Don't rush. Players sometimes lift their gloves
and start to throw before they even have the ball. Take
your time, get the ball into your glove, and only then
straighten up and make your throw.

Infielders also have the responsibility of covering their
bases and making the tag on base runners. Again,
infielders must know their jobs—what base to cover and
who to back up—before the play starts. Once the play is
under way, there is not enough time to stop and think.

**Roberto Alomar
is a smooth
fielder and may
be the best all-
around player
in the American
League.**

Playing the Outfield

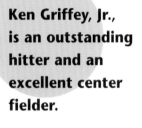

Outfielders may go inning after inning without a ball being hit to them. But when a ball does come their way, they had better be ready. A mistake in the outfield is usually a costly one. If a ball gets past an infielder, an outfielder is there as a back up. But if a ball gets past an outfielder, it usually means extra bases for the batter.

Speed and Strength

The two most important things a good outfielder needs are speed and a good arm. Speed is vital, because each of the three outfielders has to cover a lot of territory. A fast outfielder can get to a base hit and hold the batter to one base, instead of two or three. Outfielders need a strong throwing arm simply because they have to throw the ball the greatest distance of any position on the field. The throw from deep in the outfield to a **cutoff player** at midfield requires special arm strength.

Ken Griffey, Jr., is an outstanding hitter and an excellent center fielder.

Catching fly balls can be challenging at first, but with practice it does get easier.

Catching the Ball

One of the hardest outfield tasks for young players to master is judging fly balls. The easiest way to catch fly balls is to run to the spot where you think the ball will come down. Learning to judge where the ball will come down takes some practice. But you will get the hang of it. If you are in doubt about a ball, your first move should be to step back. It's always easier to correct yourself by running in on a ball than it is to run back and catch one over your head.

When running to get a ball, run on the balls of your feet, not on your heels. This keeps your head and your eyes from bouncing up and down, making it easier to see the ball. Keep your eyes on the ball as it comes down. Catch fly balls with two hands to keep the ball from bouncing out of your glove, and to put yourself in better position to throw the ball once you have it.

Pointers

Playing the outfield is easier if you keep your eyes on the ball from the moment it leaves the pitcher's hand. This helps you to tell where it's going when it's hit.

Behind the Plate

Playing catcher is a demanding job. Catchers are involved in just about every play in a game. They can get worn out from crouching and standing repeatedly during the game, and they can be battered by **foul tips** and wild pitches. On the other hand, catchers have a unique viewpoint of the game. They are in the position to look at the entire field of play. Catchers, therefore, are expected to take charge of their teams. They remind them of the number of outs, position the infielders and outfielders, and encourage their pitchers.

BASEBALL FACTS

Catchers' equipment used to be heavier and uglier than it is today. In fact, the gear used to be called the "tools of ignorance," because it left catchers so sweaty and grimy. But because the catcher has to be one of the smartest players on the team, the equipment should be called the "tools of intelligence."

In Postion

As a catcher, you should squat about an arm's length behind the batter with your weight on the balls of your feet. Hold your glove up in the batter's strike zone as a clear target for the pitcher. Your throwing hand should be behind your back. That way you won't hurt your hand on a foul tip.

Don't be afraid to stop the ball with your body. All the equipment catchers wear allows them to do just that without getting hurt.

Making Plays

One of the toughest jobs the catcher has is blocking pitches in the dirt. The idea is to keep the ball in front of you by blocking it with your body. You should drop to both knees, get your body in front of the ball, and lean your torso slightly forward. This way the ball most likely will bounce harmlessly off your chest protector and land right in front of you, where you can easily pick it up.

Catching pop-ups is another special challenge for catchers. Once the ball is hit, take off your mask and look for the ball. Once you've found the ball, throw the mask in the opposite direction, so it will be out of your way. Then run to the spot where you think the ball will come down.

Ivan Rodriguez, shown catching a foul ball, has one of the best throwing arms of any catcher in baseball.

Rules of the Game

Baseball continued to change and evolve even after Alexander Cartwright laid down the first rules in the 1840s. Even today, representatives of baseball's professional leagues gather every few years to update baseball's rule book. For example, over the last 150 years, rule changes have lengthened the distance between the pitcher and batter, made batting helmets mandatory, and outlawed the spitball. In 1973, rules in the American League were changed to allow for the designated hitter, who bats in place of the pitcher, but does not play the field.

Some rule changes reveal a lot about the way the game was once played. For much of baseball's history, players left their gloves on the playing field while their team was at bat. A thrown or batted ball that hit one of the gloves was still in play. But by the 1950s, with fielder's gloves becoming larger and posing more of a hazard, a rule was introduced making it illegal for fielders to leave their gloves laying on the ground. Today, players carry their gloves back to the dugout at the end of a half-inning.

Burleigh Grimes was the last major league pitcher allowed to throw a legal spitball. He was one of 17 pitchers allowed to continue throwing the pitch, even after it was outlawed in 1920. He pitched his last game in 1934.

Until the 1950s, some managers wore a suit and tie, instead of their team's uniform, while they worked. For example, Connnie Mack, who managed in the big leagues for 53 years, wore street clothes in the dugout. But in 1957, a new rule required base coaches to wear uniforms on the field. The rule did not say anything about managers in the dugout. But by then, wearing uniforms had become accepted practice for managers, as well.

Connie Mack, one of baseball's great managers, wore street clothes in the dugout.

In baseball's early days, a batted ball that rolled under or through the outfield fence in fair territory was ruled a home run. In fact, the first pinch-hit grand slam in American League history—by Marty Kavanagh of Cleveland in 1916—didn't fly out of the park, but rolled through a hole in the fence. After a rule change in 1931, such hits were considered ground-rule doubles.

The Birth of Baseball

Many baseball fans believe that baseball was invented by an army officer named Abner Doubleday. The **National Baseball Hall of Fame** is even located in Cooperstown, New York, where Doubleday is supposed to have developed baseball's rules. However, Doubleday had nothing to do with baseball's early development.

Baseball grew out of other bat and ball games that had been played in the United States since colonial times. If one person can be credited with "inventing" baseball as we know it today, it might be Alexander J. Cartwright. Cartwright, a surveyor and amateur athlete, laid out the dimensions of the playing field and set down the basic rules of the game. That famous 23-to-1 game played in Hoboken in 1846 was played according to Cartwright's rules.

Alexander J. Cartwright developed many of the rules by which baseball is still played.

BASEBALL FACTS

Today, fans at major-league games get to keep *home runs* and *foul balls* that are hit into the crowd. But until the 1920s, if a ball went into the stands, an usher tried to get it back. Today, big league teams go through 50 or 60 balls in a game.

Once Cartwright's rules became established, more and more baseball clubs began popping up all over the nation. The first professional baseball team, the Cincinnati Red Stockings, was founded in 1869. They toured the country that year and didn't lose a single game. By 1876, a group of professional teams had formed a league. It was called the National League and is the same National League that exists today.

Still, baseball in the 1800s was a much different game than today's baseball. Pitchers threw underhand. It took nine balls, not four, for a batter to earn a base on balls. Even the equipment was different. Fielders wore only thin leather gloves over their fielding hands. It wasn't until the 1890s that they started wearing fielding gloves like the ones we know today.

By the turn of the century, baseball was becoming ever more popular. In 1901, a second major league, the American League, was formed. Almost from the start, there was a great rivalry between the National and American leagues. In 1903, the champions of each league met in the first **World Series.** The Boston Red Sox of the American League defeated the Pittsburgh Pirates of the National League. An American tradition had begun.

By the late 1800s, baseball already closely resembled the game we know today.

Baseball's Heroes

Baseball is a great game, but it has seen its share of not-so-great times. In 1919, a group of players with the Chicago White Sox made a deal with gamblers to lose World Series games on purpose. The baseball world was shocked by what came to be known as the Black Sox scandal. Many fans lost their faith in the game.

Around the same time, a player named George Herman "Babe" Ruth was establishing himself as one of the greatest players in the history of baseball. The Babe hit the ball harder and farther than any other player. As he set about rewriting the record books for home runs, fans began flocking out to ballparks in record numbers to watch him play. It took a player as great as Babe Ruth to rescue baseball from the shame of the Black Sox scandal.

Babe Ruth's towering home runs helped make baseball wildly popular in the 1920s.

BASEBALL FACTS

The National Baseball Hall of Fame in Cooperstown, New York, honors outstanding players, such as Babe Ruth and Jackie Robinson. Election to the Hall of Fame comes only after a player has had a remarkable career. Every year, more players are elected, but only the greatest stars are considered.

But baseball was part of another scandal even more shameful than the Black Sox affair. From baseball's early days until the 1940s, team owners had agreed not to allow African-American players in the major leagues. The best black players played in the **Negro Leagues.**

One of those outstanding African-American players, Jackie Robinson, changed all of that forever. Robinson signed a contract with Branch Rickey, the general manager of the Brooklyn Dodgers, who believed that the **color barrier** was wrong. Robinson made history when he took the field for the Dodgers in 1947. But he had to put up with years of discrimination to prove that African Americans belonged in the major leagues. Robinson's courageous play proved just how ridiculous the color barrier was. Before too long, other major-league teams were signing black players.

Jackie Robinson's courage made him a hero not just to baseball fans, but to all Americans.

Today, many baseball fans believe that the game has again lost its way. They think that most players and owners are too focused on making money. In 1994, arguments between players and owners were so bad that the players refused to play. The World Series was canceled. But the past suggests that there may be another great young player waiting to rescue baseball's reputation. After all, Babe Ruth made the nation forget about the Black Sox. Jackie Robinson erased the color line.

Watching Baseball

The best way to learn about baseball is to play baseball. The second best way is to watch baseball games. Today, there are more major-league baseball teams in more cities than ever before. So now it is easier than ever to see the best players in person. New stadiums, such as Jacobs Field in Cleveland and Orioles Park at Camden Yards in Baltimore, are attracting big crowds. And many older parks, such as Wrigley Field in Chicago or Fenway Park in Boston, are small enough to allow fans to get very close to the action.

Jacobs Field in Cleveland is an example of the beautiful new parks springing up around the country.

Every baseball fan knows how exciting a towering home run can be. But some of the less visible parts of the game are just as important as the big home runs. Watching a baseball game in person reveals some of the inner workings of the game. You can see the **third-base coach** flashing signals to the batter and runners. Some of the signals may look a little silly, but they tell the batter and runner when to swing away or bunt and when to **steal a base** or stay put.

The Little League World Series is played before cheering crowds in Williamsport, Pennsylvania.

You can also watch the fielders change their positioning with each new batter—or sometimes between each pitch. Teams scout their opponents and try to anticipate where each opposing player is likely to hit the ball. Then they position their infielders and outfielders to be in the right place at the right time. No one plays the game better than major leaguers. Many of today's stars say that they learned the game by watching and imitating their favorite players. For a young player dreaming of the big leagues—or even one who is just curious about baseball—there is no more exciting way to get a feel for the game than to watch the best players at work.

BASEBALL FACTS

The first televised major-league game was played in 1939 between the Cincinnati Reds and the Brooklyn Dodgers. TV has helped to make the owners and players more money and has given fans more chances to watch their favorite teams. But it has also made it harder for smaller, minor league teams to survive. And the money has led to arguments between players and owners.

Glossary

base One of four points on a baseball field that must be touched by a runner to score a run.

base hit A hit that gets the runner to first base safely.

base on balls An award of first base to a batter who receives four pitches outside the strike zone during his or her time at bat.

base path The area between the bases within which a base runner must run. If a player is judged by the umpire to have left the base path, he or she will be called out.

batter's box The rectangle on either side of home plate, within which the batter must stand while at bat.

batting average A statistic that shows how many times a player has hit safely compared to the number of times he or she has been at bat.

bunting Trying to hit the ball softly in the infield so that the batter may reach base safely or to advance a base runner.

color barrier The unwritten agreement between major-league team owners in the first half of the 1900s excluding African-American players from the major leagues.

cutoff player A defensive player, usually an infielder, whose job is to relay throws from the outfield to one of the bases.

fastball A type of pitch delivered to get past the batter before the batter is able to make contact.

fielder's glove The most common type of baseball glove or mitt, used by infielders, outfielders, and pitchers.

foul ball A ball batted into foul territory, which is the part of the field behind home plate and across the foul lines from the infield and the outfield.

foul tip A pitched ball that is hit back toward the catcher for a foul ball. If the catcher catches a foul tip with two strikes, the batter is called out.

home run A hit that allows the batter to touch all four bases safely for a run.

lineup The list of a team's players and their positions at the start of a game.

Little League An organization that oversees youth baseball leagues and conducts an annual World Series.

major leagues The two top professional baseball leagues, the American and National.

National Baseball Hall of Fame A museum and library in Cooperstown, New York, dedicated to the history of baseball.

national pastime A name given to baseball. It refers to baseball's popularity with American sports fans over many years.

Negro Leagues A number of professional baseball leagues established for African Americans during the early 1900s in response to the exclusion of African Americans from the major leagues.

out One of three retirements of the offensive team required to end a team's turn at bat.

pitcher's rubber Sometime's called the pitching plate, a narrow platform from which the pitcher pushes off to deliver the ball to home plate.

power hitter A batter with the ability to hit many home runs or other extra base hits.

steal a base To advance by running from one base to another as a pitch is delivered to home plate.

strike A pitch that is thrown in the strike zone or swung at and missed or hit in foul territory by the batter.

strike zone The area that stretches the width of home plate and between the batter's armpits and the top of the knees.

tagging up A way for a runner to advance from one base to another. On a fly ball, the runner may wait at his or her original base for the fielder to catch the ball. Once the catch is made, he or she may try to advance to the next base.

third-base coach A coach positioned in foul territory next to third base who tells base runners when to run or stop running on batted balls.

windup The motion that begins the pitcher's delivery to the plate.

World Series The series of games played at the end of a season between the champions of the National and American leagues. The first team to win four series games wins the world championship.

Index

Baseball Records

Batting
Home runs in one season—Roger Maris, 61 (1961)
Home runs, career—Hank Aaron, 755
Batting average, career—Ty Cobb, .367
Stolen bases in one season—Rickey Henderson, 130 (1982)
Stolen bases, career—Rickey Henderson, 1,042
Hits, career—Pete Rose, 4,256
Runs, career—Ty Cobb, 2,245
Runs batted in, season—Hack Wilson, 190 (1930)
Runs batted in, career—Hank Aaron, 2,297
Bases on balls, season—Babe Ruth, 170 (1923)
Bases on balls, career—Babe Ruth, 2,056

Pitching
Wins, season—Jack Chesbro, 41 (1904)
Wins, career—Cy Young, 511
Earned run average, season—Dutch Leonard, 1.01 (1914)
Earned run average, career—Ed Walsh, 1.82
Strikeouts, season—Nolan Ryan, 383 (1973)
Strikeouts, career—Nolan Ryan, 5,668
Shutouts, season—Grover Alexander, 16 (1916)
Shutouts, career—Walter Johnson, 110
Complete games, career—Cy Young, 750